Written by Christine Lazier
Illustrated by Graham Underhill,
Pierre de Hugo, Ute Fuhr, Raoul Sautai

Specialist adviser:
Sarah Heath,
M. Phil. Conservation Policy

ISBN 1 85103 148 0
First published 1992 in the United Kingdom
by Moonlight Publishing Ltd,
36 Stratford Road, London W8
Translated by Sarah Gibson

  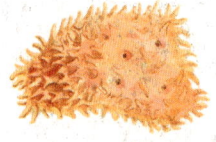

POCKET • WORLDS

Coast and Seashore

Let's explore the shoreline,
and see what we can find…

Have you ever been to the seaside?
It is a special place, where three different
environments come together: the land,
the sea and the air. Some shores are rocky,
some are sandy or muddy.
A cliff is a sheer rock face running along
the shore. From the foot of the cliffs,
the land slopes gently away out and under
the open sea.
Little by little, the cliffs are eroded by rain
and salt spray. Waves wash away pieces
of rock and break them up into shingle,
pebbles rubbed smooth and round by
the motion of the sea. In some places,
the sea pounds the rock into gravel or sand,
and spreads it all along the beaches.
Rivers also carry sand and earth down
to the sea. It collects in sheltered areas
away from the currents and turns into mud.

The sea rises and falls:
high tide and low tide.

Tides are caused when the gravitational force of the moon and the sun on the earth pulls on the surface of the oceans.

It takes the moon almost twenty-five hours to go once right round the earth, so the time of the tides gets later by about fifty minutes every day.

The sea throws up all sorts of things onto the beach: bits of seaweed, shells, starfish, pieces of wood...

In March and September the equinox
occurs. Days and nights are almost
the same length. The water rises and falls
more than usual and the tides are very high.
Life is not easy for plants and animals
on the seashore. They have to live with
the constant ebb and flow of the waves;
there's no shade from the sun's heat when
the tide is out.

They collect in a wavy line we call the 'high water mark',
which shows us how far up the beach the high tide has come.

The sand on a beach is made up
of countless tiny grains. They are mainly
pieces of a mineral called quartz, but there
are fragments of seashells as well.

Very fine sand	Ordinary sand	Coarse sand	Black sand

Plants and animals are rare on shingle beaches.
They cannot survive easily in the constantly shifting pebbles.

Sand-hoppers are crustaceans about as long
as your finger-nail which hide among
the strands of dried-up seaweed on the high
water mark. They hop up and down the
beach, following the tide, but never letting
themselves be washed away by a wave!

Flies feed on rotting
seaweed.

Sand-hoppers can cover
thirty centimetres
in one leap!

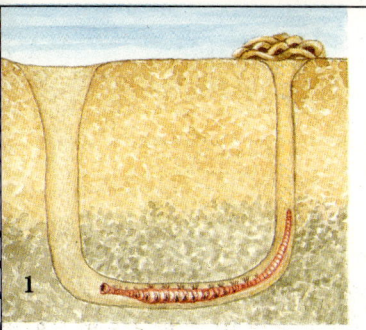
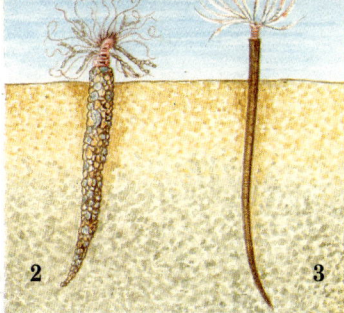

The lugworm (1), the sand mason (2) and the peacock worm (3) always stay in the same place.

At low tide, the beach may look deserted, but there are animals living in the warm, damp sand and mud. The lugworm swallows sand as it digs its tunnel. It digests any food and casts the rest in little coils on the surface. The razor shell can bury itself in the sand in less than a minute. It uses its single foot as an anchor and pulls itself down.

The razor shell (1), the cockle shell (2), the banded wedge (3) and the tellin (4) are molluscs. Their shells have two halves, called valves.

11

If you are walking over the wet sand in bare feet, watch out for the sharp spines of the weever fish. They're poisonous!

Further out, where the sand is covered by the sea, you may come across beds of eel-grass.

Many different animals live among its strands. The cuttle-fish (1) captures its prey with two tentacles, which draw the food into its mouth. If it needs to escape from a predator, it squirts out a jet of inky black liquid behind to hide in.

Smelts (2) are little fish that swim in shoals. The body of the pipefish (3) is protected by bony plates under the skin. A gilthead (4) searches for mussels to eat. A jelly-fish (5) is propelled along in jerks as it contracts its hood. The velvet swimming crab (6) has back feet that are flattened like paddles.

The plaice is a flat fish. It eats worms and little crabs which live in the sand.

4

5

1

3

6

2

Whelks eat
the remains
of other
animals.

Scallops
open and close
their shells very fast
to move along.

All around the Mediterranean coast,

there are meadows of Neptune Grass which animals use as a larder and a shelter.

A sea cucumber

At low tide, the sea anemone draws in its tentacles and closes up so that it does not dry out.

The body of this anemone is hidden inside a tube, and its tentacles wave around its mouth like plumes.

Here, the sea-hare (1) lays its eggs in long strands which fishermen call 'sea spaghetti'. The male sea-horse (2) looks after the eggs in a pouch on its abdomen until they hatch. Bass (3) and red mullet (4) scour the water in search of food. Some fish aren't such pleasant company if you are swimming. Look out for the sting-ray (5)! Its tail is armed with sharp spines. The tentacles of this jelly-fish (6) can sting you even after it is dead.

This sea-slug lives in the Pacific Ocean.

Butterfly fish

Lion fish

Angel fish

Sea-pen

In warmer seas, the animals are often more colourful. The fearsome-looking lion fish uses its huge fins as a net to trap its prey. The long spines on its back are poisonous.

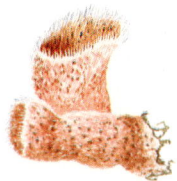

Star-fish: if one of its arms is cut off, a new star-fish can develop from it.

Sponges attach themselves to rocks. The sponge you use in the bath is the animal's soft, porous skeleton!

In the Tropics, the coasts are often fringed by coral reefs.

Coral is made by animals called polyps, whose bodies are like tiny sacks. Their skeletons pile on top of each other, forming a limestone mass.

The red coral of the Mediterranean is at risk of disappearing because of over-fishing. When it is alive, you can see the transparent tentacles of the polyps, which they use to catch their prey.

How are dunes formed?

Along flat, open coastlines where there is little shelter, the wind blows the grains of sand into mounds. Some dunes are like hills, as much as 10 metres high.

A dune on the coast of Florida. Everyday, the wind adds more sand, and gradually the dune gets bigger and shifts inland.

The plants which grow on dunes have to be able to stand up to very dry and salty conditions, sometimes even being buried in sand. Marram grass helps to stabilise the sand, and sea-holly has roots which go down 3 metres. The creeping sea-bindweed can cling on even in the strongest winds. Further into the dunes, you may find carpets of marestail grass and immortelle.

Sea purslane and golden samphire grow on the slopes of salt-marshes.

1 Sea-rocket
2 Marestail grass
3 Sea-bindweed
4 Sea-holly
5 Immortelle flower
6 Sea-aster
7 Sea-spurge

Cliffs give shelter
to all kinds of sea-birds.

In the spring, thousands of them
gather there to lay their eggs. The cliff
face rings to the cries of the adult birds
and the cheeping of their young.
The kittiwake builds a very strong
and stable nest by carefully trampling
together mud, seaweed, grass and
droppings. The puffin uses its bill
to hollow out a burrow for its eggs.
Guillemots lay a single egg
which is pear-shaped to stop
it rolling off the ledge.
Like razorbills, they are
expert underwater fishermen,
and only come to land to lay their eggs
and raise their chicks.

5

The petrel
glides just above
the surface of the waves.

1 **Kittiwake**
2 **Puffin**
3 **Guillemot**
4 **Razorbill**
5 **Shag**
6 **Gannet**

Life on a rocky coastline

At the foot of the cliffs, the rocks covered
with seaweed are home to an abundance
of shellfish. It's an excellent place
for the birds to come and find food.
The oyster-catcher alights there, turning
into the wind. He uses his beak
like pincers to dislodge
lugworms, crabs and
cockles. He prises
open their shells
to gulp down
the creatures inside.

In spite of his name, the oyster-catcher never eats oysters!

One oyster-catcher may eat as many as six hundred cockles at one low tide!
There's one bird that's never still: the turnstone hops from rock to rock or skims very fast just over the water.
It uses its strong beak to turn over the seaweed and pebbles in search of the molluscs, crustaceans or insects hiding underneath.

The turnstone is strong enough to turn over stones as heavy as he is!

The animals cling on very tightly where the rocks are pounded by the waves!

The limpet has a foot which acts as a sucker and allows the animal to glide over the rock to graze on seaweed.

Acorn barnacles, on the other hand, do not move a millimetre.

Where the water is calmer, you will find lichens and many different kinds of seaweed.

Bladder wrack

Acorn barnacle

Mussel covered with barnacles

Ormer

Yellow lichen　　**Black lichen**　　**Flat wrack**　　**Periwinkle**

Mussels attach themselves to rocks with byssus, hair-like strands produced from a gland in their foot. When they move, they fix new threads onto the rock from one side and break the old ones.

Edible winkle　　**Chiton shell**　　**Limpet**　　**Topshell**

When the tide goes out, it leaves little pools behind in hollows and crevices in the rocks.
Have you ever watched a sea-urchin (1) moving along? If you're lucky, you might see a star-fish using its arms to open a shell.

A crab scuttles sideways from under some sea-weed. The hermit-crab (2) borrows the shell of another animal to protect its soft and vulnerable body.

What is seaweed?

An aquatic plant which does not
have separate flowers, leaves
or roots. Instead, it has a thallus.
Some seaweeds drift, others fix
themselves to rocks and shells
with a holdfast. Several kinds
are edible.

Sugar kelp or 'sea-belt' fixes itself
to rocks or shells in places which
are never exposed
by the tide.

Sea Lettuce

Bladder wrack:
the blisters pop
if you squeeze them.

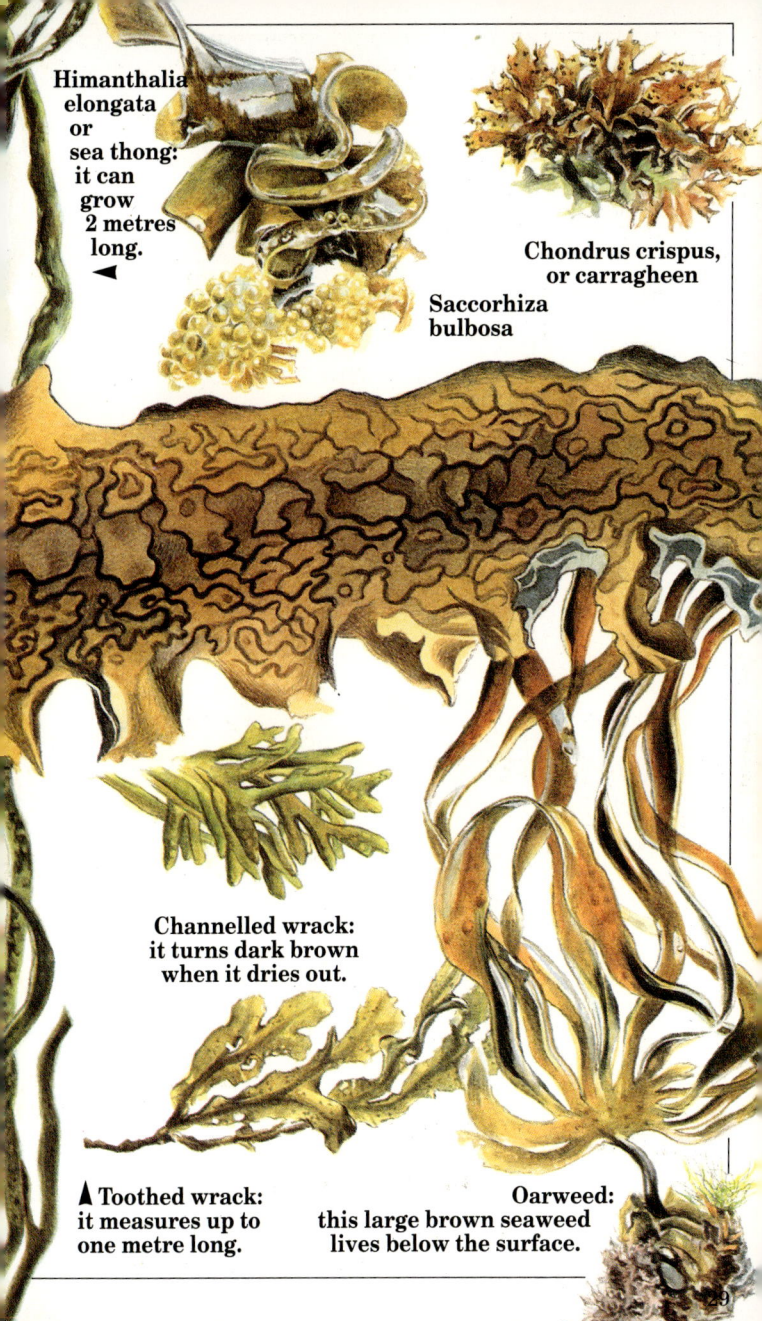

Himanthalia elongata or sea thong: it can grow 2 metres long. ◄

Chondrus crispus, or carragheen

Saccorhiza bulbosa

Channelled wrack: it turns dark brown when it dries out.

▲ Toothed wrack: it measures up to one metre long.

Oarweed: this large brown seaweed lives below the surface.

The mouth of a river is called an estuary.
Here, the muddy, fresh water of the river
mingles with the salt sea water.
The mud sinks
to the bottom.
The animals that live
in an estuary are adapted
to water that is half fresh,
half salty.

In some bays, young oysters are raised
in oyster farms on tiles covered with sand.
They fix themselves to the tiles
with a sort of cement which they secrete
from the outer edge of their skin, or mantle.

The common shore crab likes the muddy
sea bed but you may also catch sight of one
on the sand or rocks. If it senses danger,
it rears up, stretches out its claws and
clacks one against the other, making
as much noise as it can. More often, it will
just disappear into the mud and hide.

**Certain sea mammals live in estuaries too: you may well
see common seals lying out on the sand banks at low tide.**

**The redshank, a wader, spends
its winters on estuaries.**

The macaque monkey eats crabs.

In the Tropics, on coasts where the water is calm or at the mouth of a river, a weird forest may grow, called a mangrove swamp. Mangroves trees grow closely together, with their feet in the salty water. Their arching roots make some of them look as though they are perched on stilts.

The enormous claw of the fiddler crab is not as dangerous as it looks! The male waves it about to entice the female from her burrow.

Snakes and monkeys live in the branches
of the mangroves and, down in the water,
crocodiles wait motionless for their prey.
Macaque monkeys chase crabs
across the sand at low tide.

Slip on your boots or your rubber shoes and pick up a basket. There are so many things to find and look at when the tide is out.

You could collect shells, or pebbles of every colour and pattern, polished smooth by the sea. There will be hundreds of them in the sand.

But remember, never collect live animals – only pick up empty shells.

Guess which shellfish hide in these holes in the sand: a razor shell, a cockle shell or a tellin?

The razor shell leaves two holes very close together.

The cockle shell leaves two holes slightly apart.

The tellin leaves two holes clearly separated.

How can you tell whether limpets have moved? Lightly draw round their outlines with nail varnish. Put a different mark on each limpet and the line you have drawn around it. After the next tide, come back and see which ones have moved.

Index

Pocket Worlds – building up into a child's first encyclopaedia: